THE PORTAGE POETRY SERIES

SERIES TITLES

Lake, River, Mountain
Mark B. Hamilton

Talking Diamonds
Linda Nemec Foster

Poetic People Power
Tara Bracco (ed.)

The Green Vault Heist
David Salner

There is a Corner of Someplace Else
Camden Michael Jones

Everything Waits
Jonathan Graham

We Are Reckless
Christy Prahl

Always a Body
Molly Fuller

Bowed As If Laden With Snow
Megan Wildhood

Silent Letter
Gail Hanlon

New Wilderness
Jenifer DeBellis

Fulgurite
Catherine Kyle

The Body Is Burden and Delight
Sharon White

Bone Country
Linda Nemec Foster

Not Just the Fire
R.B. Simon

Monarch
Heather Bourbeau

The Walk to Cefalù
Lynne Viti

The Found Object Imagines a Life: New and Selected Poems
Mary Catherine Harper

Kevin Thomason's masterful and moving poetry collection, *Even the Sky*, is drawn taut as a canvas. With keen observance, these poems follow the vivid horizon of the line and never "lets the looker look away." Crafted with concision and care, Thomason's lyric vision saturates every page, leaving the reader with an afterimage of its potent humanity.

—AMY FLEURY
author of *Sympathetic Magic*

Kevin Thomason writes poems that are hard to forget. In a time when nuance seems at a ridiculous low, this book delights in what's most often overlooked. There's something here that reminds me of a young Goethe. And it was Goethe who said, "You don't have to travel around the world to understand the sky is blue everywhere." Thomason reminds us, though, it's more complicated than that. There are a million shades of blue, and it's always dawn, or dusk, or midnight somewhere. These poems are stunning in their complexities. *Even the Sky* is a sublime debut.

—MICHAEL SHEWMAKER
author of *Leviathan*

In Kevin Thomason's absorbing and timely collection, *Even the Sky*, memory doesn't console—it complicates those "angles and errors" of the hoped-for and the disappointed, "the patchwork of our parents' talk." Uneasy inheritances, for sure—family sagas, mythologies, the pictures we pass down. As Thomason writes in a sonnet called "The Extra Room," what would it mean to start again at the "accomplishment of nothing's details," the great quiescence of it all? What would it mean to think like the next sunrise—"that never expects us"?

—COLLIER BROWN
author of *Scrap Bones*

Even the Sky
poems

Kevin Thomason

CORNERSTONE PRESS
UNIVERSITY OF WISCONSIN-STEVENS POINT

Cornerstone Press, Stevens Point, Wisconsin 54481
Copyright © 2025 Kevin Thomason
www.uwsp.edu/cornerstone

Printed in the United States of America

Library of Congress Control Number: 2025940335
ISBN: 978-1-960329-95-0

Cornerstone Press titles are produced in courses and internships offered by the
Department of English at the University of Wisconsin–Stevens Point.

DIRECTOR & PUBLISHER
Dr. Ross K. Tangedal

EXECUTIVE EDITORS
Jeff Snowbarger, Freesia McKee

EDITORIAL DIRECTOR
Brett Hill

SENIOR EDITOR
Ellie Atkinson

PRESS STAFF
Sophie McPherson, Ava Willett, Madison Schultz, Karlie Harpold, Mydasia
Zipperer, Autumn Vine, Allison Lange

—*for Deborah*

CONTENTS

1. Diversion

2. Zero Speaks

3. The Art Machine

4. Easements

5. Silent Films

1

Diversion

Burglary

Find a house with a tar-crisp fringe
of shingles, an ardent roof's warped edge
sloping from the clean sky. Below,
an incidental porch, I hope,
espouses plants from spidery twine.
You'll need an egg-yolk yellow light
at a drawn shade's corner. Test
the creaking of the gate, yes.

And now the most important matter:
scale its bricks or bring a ladder.
Steal, then, to a windowpane's reflection.
In the moon's marred glow, slip detection
till the day comes, and you are gone,
bedded down in the teal-dark lawn.

Groundskeeper

Over the anonymous graves, he breaks
    their markers loose from guesswork's
reckoned earth. He could confuse them when he rakes,
    each stake as white as a saucer,
but each will lean, one by one, along the fence
    till only an acre exists
with its surety of grass and clover
    to cover the designs of dirt.

    But no one marks this extra chore
or grasps the hour in which he reconstructs
    every row as it was before.
You might have watched him loading up his truck
    or noticed when he drove away.
You swear you know his name but couldn't say.

Diversion

Too often it's the one grace that saves us.
Some babe bends her finger at goons
by the exit—buffed-up hunks with hard faces
and pistols at their thighs. She reaches and swoons.

Or some kid shouts, *Hey, asshole! Over here!*
while the rest escape once the coast is clear.
Other times an apple thuds against the wall
or firecrackers blow up in a stall.

But a pay phone tells us we must choose:
Save yourself or save the town. Clues
planted for us lead toward the wrong shack.
A pillow's tied to the railroad track.
Walk into a trap, and there's no walking free.
Our weapons down, someone counts to three.

Description of a Hall of Columns

They couldn't mark its style of column.
Gapping ridges armored each curve
and ribbed them in shadows. *Solemn
yet open*—but they had no nerve
to write their graceless sentence.
Who could walk the groves of stone within?
They dared pictures from a distance
and slept in town, meaning to begin
every next day. They tried to ask
who built this wonder. None could say.
Villagers whispered about their task
and knew the hall would have its way.
They, too, penciled architecture
and dreamt of strangers they could lecture.

Camera Angles

Opening: Aerial Shot

What summons this rush of skyline, margins
of bundled hills, buildings, and clouds; this largesse
of miniature, stubbed to echo notes of lost
height's hollows; the drags of shadow tossed
on low roads; ache in these hefts and recesses
that situate as distance regresses;
this loose grip of approach the moment wields,
poised as if balanced on a fence, that yields
the presence of characters below,
as if there were other places they go?

Closing: Pull–Back Shot

This scenery where the scene retreats
pulls back until the frame completes
an ending that's never in doubt:
a white flag above a redoubt,
nets dropped on toughs and cronies,
sundry wedding ceremonies.
This is insistence to make sense.
This is the forgiveness tense,
that lets the looker look away,
that lets the credits have their say.
The quiet might as well be loud,
an exit in the shape of a crowd
dismissing through the double doors.
Someone stays to sweep the floors.

In Defense of Melodrama

The world performs on a single stilt,
a tedious spin on a drastic tilt.

Balance askew, attentions demand
simple plots that the simple understand.

Sprung up by sudden string music, all scenes
cue before painted skies and greens.

Characters flatten as Mortimers and Claras
mistake each other for Sterlings and Sarahs.

Action rises by preposterous design.
The sidekick trips or something's wrong with the wine.

Beams collapse and villains break through,
the scenery behind them still green, still blue.

A Boy's Supplication

He feels them now begin to fall—
the voice and breath of night air
about the house. Someone still talks.
He cannot quiet creaks in stairs
or the drumbeat drip of broken sinks.
As light fades to the shutting door,
the room folds over him like wings
of crows. The weight of night is sure.

A last restraint of gravity
allows the ceiling fan to spin
in gestures of solemnity,
showing again again again
how to whisper away the wind.

Unstoppable Force Meets Immovable Object

Margin for error means one of us wins,
but, lately, our meetings haven't meant much.
Shorelines slink at surfers, and a boulder
slips loose at a grunt. Leviathans
budge, these days, for any prophet's hunch.
Façades flinch from a long stare.
Decree and denial have nothing to spare.

But somewhere a tower won't tip over
because awestruck mudslides refuse to spill.
Gales ungather and tremors condense.
Pendulums waver to a standstill.
Gravity depends. Voices pray
as soldiers crawl toward a fence.
Between us—it could go either way.

Two Interpretations of *Laocoön and His Sons*

I.

You know this famous sculpture,
even if you haven't seen it.
A man abated by his pose
of batting off bands of snakes.
Worse, his boys, all knees and elbows,
baroque in frozen jerks and shakes.
One more "not-okay" family to endure.
Assume the turd was hurled, the fan hit.

Forget about the Trojan War—
and that Laocoön wasn't wrong
about the Greek horse left on the shore.
And who cares why the sons belong?
They tried to stay, they tried to run.
They're family, an enduring one.

II.
My dad, too, would think the horse was weird
and have me listen for an oaken heart.
He'd smile till a frown appeared,
and then we'd load it in our cart.
Staring into its nostrils, I would dread
his words and brush the flanks again.
Strangeness always finds its kindred,
he'd say. Not hard to imagine.

Silence measures the miles we ride
carting our secret down the road,
endless gray slate we watch side by side
but never a place to unload.
We stare ahead until, like I feared,
I start to think the horse is weird.

2

Zero Speaks

The Story of a Liar

Trees lean into themselves today.
Sun stands in the way of shade,

but the wind eases branches down
to shadow's soft resolve of ground,

as if they bend for leaves that drop
while more spill from the top.

Signatures

i. Signature Practice

Nestle the kind of lacework erasers wreathe,
those hairline loops only a hand can weave.
Secret as the ink on 20s, slip a dot
above an i and a paraph underneath
its ligatured slopes. Savor this slick dance
of design, its letters locked in brisk stance,
and the mere gist that jots up this knot—
whatever license, loan, or chance
your steady and practiced hand has got.

ii. Signature Line

Seal the agreement at its edge,
where meaning lets down to this ledge
that prompts a delicate eye. Squint
to guide what purchase you'll draw. Wedge
a tree line's contours into view,
shafts of emptiness leaking through
reach and crag. Mean what you meant.
Drag the pen till boundaries are true.
Explain, if you can, where they went.

iii. No One's Signature

Reckon its want careless indeed,
its lustered script too artful to read
in this codex a dozen times glossed.
Witness the serifs curl and recede.
Discern such cursive occurrence
purl to a squirrelly tassel once
it fixes for disappearance,
the measure of commitment's cost—
date imprecise, author long lost.

Having Words

Those bags of silence
stuffed in back won't do.
Don't they need to be
unpacked, sorted through?
To say what should be
said, words should come

quick as coughs, loud breaths,
or crumpled paper
to a bin. Or soon
planes drag banners of
them overhead.

Below, we bend our
necks, squint to read them
as they waver, and
then repeat what

they surely don't mean.
Now leaflets drift down.
Evacuate

or die. Fine, we think.
We'll go. Our bags

are packed.

Zero Speaks

It's not that I'm nothing, no,
just the nothing that blunders
beyond—stomach on a stick figure,
gap of a missed zipper,
quickie she wished had been quicker.

All the integers abut but me.
Unrehearsable number
going on at once. Where I'm from,
I'm the nothing that nothing entertains,
the cosmic rattling of shit for brains.

Find me in rings that ride out
to calmness on a lake face.
But I'm the plunk of the rock
that struck it, the butt-head, the bore,
punk ass mooning you from the shore.

Changes to an Abandoned Landscape

April

It comes as if it can't be seen,
a sense that settles in the upset
grass, that must have burst from seeds
and breaths of coughed winter air,
an absence of boll and bark and ear,
those sheaves of witness to what was:
clear awns and unflawed rinds.

October

Stray sprigs of crops remain.
Copses for autumn cordwood,
grim as ancient statues,
screen an unfenced graveyard
lost like days are lost
to grief. I gather what I find—
offshoots of the very same vines.

December

No descendant's goats bleating
at the remnants of the weeds
graze these greenless plots.
The field's flourishing of absence
spreads in bits of twigs and trash,
cruelty lacing the nests of crows—
terrain where anything grows.

The Hill I'm Dying On

Below this hill
on which I'm dying,
for miles, others
are surviving.

Squared homes fill up
city grids,
cornered to raise
laughter and kids.

Ingenious lights
and signs in sync
with everything
their people think.

Intersections
at every street
with crosswalk signals
that repeat:

as one person walks,
another soon stands
until given
that command.

Baseball, 1951

Sid, of course, had said to watch every swing,
had said that each pitch was like a chance.

The field, to me, was a ceaseless scatter
of green, the players working along lines

I couldn't see. And my mother-in-law's hat
was in my face when I turned to home plate;

only the bound-up beads and blue
feather overlaying a citrus brim

were in view. Sid said something would happen
soon, keep watching. Other wives—some husbands too—

eyed the vendors and the dugout and the signs.
He explained the pitcher's stance, positions,

the infield fly rule. Then, a shoulder
touching mine swayed. Seats creaked as someone's shoe

behind me tapped along and stopped. *Did you
see that? Did you, honey?* And we all stood

and cheered and sat back down. *You were looking right
at the play*, he said. *I didn't miss it*,

I lied, but just as I'd gathered myself
enough to look at him again, a man

with a camera walked by. *Give us a smile*,
he said. My mother-in-law did.

Three Studies of New Shoes

Left-foot, name-brand loafer
found on highway shoulder—
sacrificial altar
where the lost await rewards—
with abandoned Ford
and Jesus billboard.

~

High-heels, oak-bark brown,
kept dormant in box,
beneath tawny gown
never pulled down—
maturing among flip-flops,
tennis shoes, and socks.

~

Sneakers on school floor,
their too-blue allure
on this fungus-gray grid,
worn by a kid
taking up the door,
learning how he did.

The Auction Shed

This is where sour grapes or tough love brings
the lost and written off: trailered cars,
grosses of t-shirts, and stringless guitars.
Never the pedigreed and graded things
displayed in parlor cabinets like remains—
a Stone Age statuette or hunting knife,
the likeness of some bearded colonel's wife,
or tapestries depicting Charlemagnes.

Still, it's worth a lot for the one who wins.
These takers don't smartly cough as they raise
numbered paddles to hail the auctioneer.
They don't pretend not to care when it ends.
A silence settles from the static's haze
of shouts and sighs—a silence loud and clear.

3

The Art Machine

Butchering Scenes, Tomb of Prince Mentuemhat,

–c.680–650 B.C. Egyptian, late Dynasty 25–early Dynasty 26

This is no triptych of some tempted saint,
no self-portrait of a post-war painter.
Here's simple human hardness: cuts of stone
slabbed for three scenes of a sacrificed calf.
Its placard tells no more than what is shown.
Still, the craftsman knew to draw our gaze
away from those lotions of afterlife
embalmers pour from the beast's unpacked parts:
lines of sight curve towards the killer, the praised
butcher reminding us that this is art,
that slaughter's craft is just a canvas carved.
He decides what to keep and what to cut,
ensures the dead won't wake, decay, or starve—
and lifts a knife above the prince's gut.

The Art Machine

Three testaments from the height of its influence

1. The Inventor

The hand harbors what it engineers.
Sketching only shaped my inner ache
    for templates stricter than designs
allowed, the dizzied schema that clouds make
    and remake. A pencil draws lines
never straighter than its form appears.

    But merely breathing molds glass
from air and grit, and a dancer blows fire
    with a rinse of fuel and the breath's
blunt function. Crowds don't gather to admire
    such flare; they muse on the body's depths—
those darknesses measured by days we pass—

    where substance lengthens to the place
of our blueprints, which no pencil can trace.

2. The Machinist

I really must withhold my name,
though I understand little but its gears
    and frame. When they come, volunteers—
the machine's art—seem tense, as if disguised,
    like faces in mirrors, recognized
reversed but who, somehow, don't look the same.

    I only run its programmed schemes.
And its pieces grow, some say, more arcane,
    and some fall strange before its stone,
as bent as bodies bend. I can't explain.
    They take on poses of their own,
then gaze for hours, stilled in sun-stirred dreams.

    They sometimes turn from staring and smile.
I pretend to read a gauge, move a dial.

3. The Curator

The highest work of our machine
wears a snowstone dress against her paleness,
    and my face reddens, I confess,
when I retouch her gibbous cheeks. Obscene

    as some think it—she gets her way.
Her statued posture reaches to persuade
    with the last movement she made;
her lips hold the next word she would say.

    But what, then, am I taken with
as I fix her to the floor? Lights awaken
    from hidden shafts, her arabesque
heightened by its shadows about the plinth.
    Soon, I feel, a tear will break
from her eye—and she'll dab it with her wrist.

Lienzo de Tlaxcala

The lecturer circles to a projector
and corrects its touch against an unfazed wall.
Figures unfuzz in the shock of pause
which a battle's come to. From its pitch,
sunk to the lull of the last alive,
delicate men, strained from the stride
of horses or the hefts of swords, close in

on what's now only a crowd of grins
caught in the anguish of the stilled, unwaved
in a wind of stasis that won't carry
their meaning off and won't blink the eyes
enthralled. Scholars say they turn their faces
a certain way. This one asks, *Questions,
anyone?* and moves along to *the woman*

you'll notice in the midst of what's gone on.
For the students, once she's there, she's all
that's there, a character who lived too long ago
for them to care or not care, till classroom
darkness yields the ceiling's shore at the crests
of their nods and specks of corners to spot
if outside doesn't fill the window first.

Color is vital here, too. Browns of trunks,
sashes of blue, feathers rubbed powder red,
and gun-weighted grays unfocus again.
Bands of cloud, sand, and ground bleed
together as the speaker glares in the square
of canary light shot from his machine,
which he shakes and curses and reloads.

Ledger of Joseph

—"...he left numbering; for it was without number."
Genesis 41:49

Forget how ears and kine were counted
seven plenties and seven famines:
we always wonder what might happen—
wind-raw stalks and pecks of drought,
a blackleg and bloated herd.
What skill can solve a scry of dreams?
He couldn't conjure from slain sheep,
augured no clutters of blackbirds.
The mean of true and false, he learned
was miracle. In ledgers dreamt,
he tallied pharaoh, god, and myth,
foretold how lack blooms the yields
abundance blinds us to. Remember,
his brothers bound the boy away.
He'd slept and seen their sheaves lain,
seen them dimmed among the splendor
of Heaven. From the pit that gaped
his family's lie, certain now the art
of being right, he summed the stars
until a figure took its shape.

4

Easements

Black-and-White Photograph of a Relative

Edges cut strange
shadows this time of day.
As sunlight strays,
roof shade falls short
on the porch, its doorway
a slate-black slab behind
a crouched man. Contrast
dominates the scene
in dual grains of age
that resist one another.
Trees abate themselves
in ashen air, their blades
and pools of light crossed
no more in the give
and take of wind.
Branches stain the bitter,
pale spates of sky
that separate them. The cabin's
contours soften under
scrutiny till a blotted
onyx form remains.
Nightfall hesitates
at the backdrop's wan
broadness, absence locked
in its momentous failure
to arrive, unable to fade,
unable to clarify.

Ampersand

In carved hearts—the artery,
link that links but won't
spell it out, scarf for pairs
of playwrights, proprietors'
handshakes, clique twixt
neon names, evenness
on invites, bend that brings
us back to the one who
brought us, the curve
of my dad's hand for come on
just don't get in the way.

Tall for His Age

Lithe but lunking, when I slunk
a desk cracked up. My legs jutted
out like kickstands. My arms
sulked from shirtsleeves cinched
too short and the nonsense of my neck
that sloped in dismissal. In crowds,
I strode like a pair of scissors.

I came from the suburb's other side
and trudged from school past bushes
and the butter-colored paint of brick
to get back, boulevards where poplars
propped in mulch lined the walks
of glass green lawns, their boughs
like yardsticks above my awkward height.

In the blame of quiet, roads thinned
the farther I went. Trucks filed by
in sunlight that paled the grass
and stained banks of ponds in brown shade.
A grove swelled with ash tree gray
till sheens of dusk powdered down
and dimmed my face. Exposed roots

shouldered up from the turf like figures
carved in relief, and weed bunches
shot through, slanting across
my shins. Over messes of logs
and twigs, limbs lowered veils
of vine threads. Mushrooms
and long-petaled sprouts hunkered.

Trunk after trunk troubled
the ground and then ceased before
a breach of houses, orbed over

with evening and out-of-whack
like my demeanor, hands jammed
in pockets, head a dull bulb,
tall for my age, but not enough.

Putting Winter Clothes Away

At last, he'd truck them up
to the attic in tubs,
our wads of cardigans
and coats ignored since March
and his few winter shirts
I'd wear later, their colors
laced in plaids or patterned
with scattered ovals and flecks,
hues like clay, dripped honey,
curls of bark stripped away.
Bedroom windows cast
what remained of the sky's
breadth of tan, our days
lengthening out of hand.

Cozy Murder Mystery

The sound of an exit
quickens out of frame.
We see only the wreck
of a body displayed,
the rock of a wallet
still in its pocket,
cuff links somehow buttoned,
shirttail unruffled.

Cut to a party.
A woman reads a note,
covers her heart
from its ominous quote,
and rises to her guests.
We're all suspects,
one of them says,
even you, Agnes.

The shot pans to a door.
Someone is gone.
A clock flaunts the hour.
A mark on the desk, a shawl.
It's all there—
minutiae of hair,
shoe patterns in dust,
blood on a dead man's bust.

My Father's Scarecrows

He always needed something else
to do the trick. Chips of soap
swayed as dulled wind chimes, and buckets
cupped hair in the soil. Pie pans
flopped from stobs like falling hats
to pop at the calmest nudge. Shoes
hung from branches by their tongues.

I couldn't tell if rabbits burrowed
by the rick or deer puddled
across our ditch.
                            Enough,
he'd say, *hold this*, and tied back
tomato vines with cloth soaked
in pepper sauce or wolf piss.
It doesn't matter what it is.

Miniatures

032a—097c
See townsfolk fixed in busyness,
their attitudes in blunt accord,
workers attired in their dependence
on the moment they're working toward.

> *043b*
> Find a postman crouched before
> the shape of a postal sack
> to begin his suburban tour
> or finish and make his way back.

> *058b, 059a, 059b, 059c*
> Downtown streets model
> the fine detail of disrepair.
> A squatter croons into his bottle
> that others wait for him to share.

074b
And there's a painter in overalls
applying a coat of white
to green graffiti on the walls,
the letters higher than his height.

> *091d, 092a*
> This woman bends to a Corvette
> window, where she cups a match
> before her slender cigarette.
> The driver waits for it to catch.

035a, 036b
Forests buffer the outskirts
of town, where gated houses loom.
Meet a husband grinning till it hurts
and a wife who never leaves her room.

Second Marriage

Where they've argued
in the yard, evening
works its calm
around tools
plunked in chops
of grass. The porch
sticks out like a jaw.
On the clothesline,
a white shirt stills,
falters, and re-begins
its awkward halting
in the wind,
while a bra, nearly
loosened, flurries
in delay. A voice
calls the dog,
who comes at once.
Words are not
repeated much.

Easements

No one skinny-dipped or camped
in woods that bordered our clump
of houses, but we'd heard that weirdos
snuck sophomores and beers—
far from where they lived—
in the glen where cars could fit.

We halted at the posted sign:
Trespassers Fined
hung near a grassy-edged gap
in close-grown oaks, the habits
of squirrels and birds overhead
loud and strengthening as we left.

When evening's daily ton
of gray tinged the ground,
we waited for porch sounds
stripped to the starkest tone.
Tires came to a gravelly stop.
As footsteps eased up a stoop,

a screen door scudded and squawked.
The patchwork of our parents' talk,
its angles and errors a pattern
we troubled ourselves to unlearn,
called us even closer. No one
went back—and called it fun.

5

Silent Films

The Extra Room

A quiver of what's wrong steadies to a stop
in the uneasy neatness of these drapes,
so quick and lost at the baseboard's grip.
There, a wall leads to an entrance agape
at the accomplishment of nothing's details:
a ceiling fan's pose, a tossed shoe,
a blanket wrapped in itself like something
sworn, an agitation that came before.

Beautiful when the room's grandest piece,
stillness, starts back. For the comfort
of who comes, it remains long after they leave.
Its revelry against the door's impolite thrust
is a sound hardly there before it ends,
or so someone in the house pretends.

Stanzas

An attic, an office—we thought we wanted room,
but the shape of our house withheld its spare room.

Surprised by a field full of the moon,
chamber for the heart's unshared room.

Caves carve themselves from echoes of your voice.
Closed off, a whisper blares in all that room.

A skyscraper escapes even the sky,
from here on the tenth floor, left side, last room.

One man reaches for another, but it's me
wiping a mirror clean, never touching the room.

They say I'll find my name taped on my door;
a ridge of torn paper means this room is yours.

Loose Change

Not loose like chains
or laces, the coins
that cleaning recovers,
gobbled by cushion gaps
or the grot of a pocket
and wheeled in oil and grit.

Doughtier than most
that gets forgotten,
they garner in the corners
of a drawer's disarray
or blend with the dust
of a sun-starched floorboard

and wait, their teeny measure
hyperbolic. More and more
often, I just toss them,
their sputter through trash
like water's harried spill,
like words lost in the mouth's

hollow, better off swallowed,
this treasure of some nether
side, where day after
day's braid of ellipsis
never misses such amounts,
where exactness clusters

like a sum of clouds, humble
in salt-white plainness,
columns of pennies perfect
on dressers, unthwacked piggy
banks savored, trash
heaps rich with remainders.

Bury Me with Bad Men

—a silent film

We never hear the unfamiliar birdsong
that wakes her, dawn sudden with piccolo
and flute notes stirring as if the sun was wrong
in rising.
                    It's not for us to know
the clicking of her steps at every street,
and not the alley for the private phrase,
and not the city's hour on repeat.

We only watch as the music plays
and turn our heads, like the time that you
couldn't hear me, and I couldn't hear you.

Pantry Door

Remember when I jammed the pantry door?
For me, it was a long but good day,
pulling and prying it out of the way,
like something unsaid we needed to say
was stuck and we didn't care what came before
the day I jammed the pantry door.

Aubade

Nature anticipates disaster.
Birds abscond through doubling
orange light, seepages
of lower scarlet layers
curtailed by clouds and blended
in frail cerulean. Even
leaves shift louder
than wind flaws warrant
in the mountain gaps' margins
of scarce violet, where rock
faces respond to the warmth
in uniform reserve,
erosion's elder gesture
slimming them to sheerer
drops beyond reckoning.
Mere presence confounds
forever. The fineries of sprigs
and nameless tufts awe
at this embrittled hour
when yellow blanches beige
and shadows exchange grays
for deeper darks beneath
relief, from petal and stem
to stone ledge until,
at last, sunrise scatters
to a full sky, an increment
of cover that's endless
and never expects us.

ACKNOWLEDGMENTS

Grateful acknowledgment is made to the following publications in which some of these poems first appeared:

32 Poems: "Ledger of Joseph"

Angle: "Butchering Scenes, Tomb of Prince Mentuemhat"

Arkansas Review: "My Father's Scarecrows," "Groundskeeper"

The Best American Poetry blog: "Black-and-White Photograph of a Relative"

Measure: "A Boy's Supplication"

Southern Poetry Review: "Diversion"

Raleigh Review: "Zero Speaks"

Terrain.org: "Second Marriage"

Narrative Magazine: "Ampersand"

Valparaiso Poetry Review: "The Auction Shed"

I'm sincerely grateful to Dr. Ross Tangedal at Cornerstone Press for his patience, commitment, and kindness. Thanks to Brett Hill, Karlie Harpold, Mydasia Zipperer, and the rest of the editorial staff for their careful workmanship with this manuscript.

A great deal of thanks goes to the Center for Writers at the University of Southern Mississippi for the friendships and guidance I found there. I'm forever indebted to the community of McNeese State University. Its ever-growing family of writers is responsible for so much support, camaraderie, and richness in my life.

I'd like to express my deep gratitude to those who, over the years, encouraged the writing of these poems: John Bensko, James Brasfield, Rita Costello, Neil Connelly, Joyce Inman, Adam Clay, Joshua Bernstein, and Ery Shin. Special thanks to Angela Ball for lessons in serious play and to Amy Fleury for writing the beautiful trouble of this world.

Many thanks to my friends for their generosity and care, especially Gerard Duncan Jr., Adam Moore, and Michael Shewmaker for reading draft after draft of these poems, and to Jordan Ross, Nick Racz, Devin Conner, Drew Paslay, Scott Thomason, Allie Mariano, Joel Ferdon, and Rachael Fowler for always asking how the writing was going. I'm so grateful to Stephanie Seavers for her belief in me. I'm lost at how to thank my friend Keagan LeJeune enough, but I might as well be lost in a place that matters.

I owe so much, not least my appreciation for words, to my family: to my mom and dad for everything they taught me about love, to my grandparents for their unyielding support, and to Courtney, Grace, and Luke for their encouragement and laughter.

And to Deborah, for all of our camping in the middle of nowhere and matches struck unexpectedly in the dark: I've seen so much because of you, I love you.

KEVIN THOMASON is from Memphis, Tennessee and has lived in Canada and South Korea. His work can be read in *Narrative Magazine, Arkansas Review, Southern Poetry Review,* and elsewhere. His poem, "Black-and-White Photograph of a Relative," was featured online by *The Best American Poetry.* He's also written work on commission for design projects. He teaches in the MFA program at McNeese State University and travels back and forth between Lake Charles, Louisiana, and Memphis, where his wife, Deborah Elam, works as a graphic designer.